LAST SUPPERS

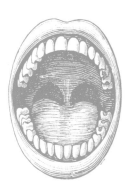

LAST SUPPERS

a Collection OF

FINAL MEALS

THROUGH *the* YEARS

CAROLINE WEST & MARK LATTER

DOG 'n' BONE

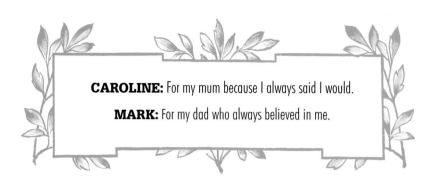

CAROLINE: For my mum because I always said I would.

MARK: For my dad who always believed in me.

Published in 2014 by Dog 'n' Bone Books
An imprint of Ryland Peters & Small Ltd
20–21 Jockey's Fields, London WC1R 4BW
519 Broadway, 5th Floor, New York, NY 10012

www.rylandpeters.com

10 9 8 7 6 5 4 3 2 1

Text © Caroline West/Mark Latter 2014
Design © Dog 'n' Bone Books 2014

A CIP catalog record for this book is available from
the Library of Congress and the British Library.

ISBN: 978 1 909313 40 8

Printed in China

Editor: Caroline West
Designer: Mark Latter

For digital editions, visit www.cicobooks.com/apps.php

CONTENTS

Introduction

In our day-to-day lives, food is vital to each and every one of us, giving so much more than simply sustenance and nourishment. Food is a source of reassurance, too, with many of us turning to special comfort foods, like chocolate and cake, or favorite family dishes, in times of need or distress. At social gatherings and events, sitting down to a meal together provides an opportunity to chat, laugh, reinforce familiar bonds, and, most of all, enjoy eating.

It's a little ironic then that this life-giving food should be such a common factor in death, from food-centered wakes after funerals to final acts of kindness shown to condemned death-row prisoners who are allowed to choose a last meal before facing execution.

"Come along inside... we'll see if tea and buns can make the world a better place."

(from *The Wind in the Willows* by Kenneth Grahame)

"Cauliflower is nothing but cabbage with a college education."

Mark Twain (American author, 1835–1910)

Today, the western world is spoiled for choice with food; we can literally buy and eat whatever we want, whenever we want. We all have our favorite foods, both good and bad, but have you ever thought what you would ask for if you only had one final meal before shuffling off this mortal coil? Hard, isn't it? Many people (famous and otherwise) who feature in *Last Suppers* had absolutely no idea they had just eaten their last meal, either dying tragically in unforeseen disasters or suddenly as the result of ill-health. Some just partied too hard… and paid the price, never knowing that what they last ate would go down in history.

 What would yours be?

"I did not get my SpaghettiOs,
I got spaghetti, I want the
press to know this."

THOMAS GRASSO
(1960–1995, DEATH ROW PRISONER)

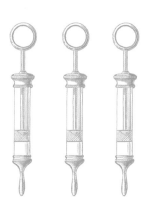

DEATH ROW

DEAD MEN WALKING

IT IS TRADITION, PERHAPS AS A LAST ACT OF HUMANITY, FOR CONDEMNED PRISONERS TO REQUEST A FINAL MEAL AND RECEIVE THE LAST RITES, IF REQUESTED, BEFORE FACING THEIR INEVITABLE DEATH.

DEATH ROW FACTS

OVER 1,300 offenders have
been sentenced to death in
the United States since 1976.

LETHAL INJECTION CONSISTS OF...

SODIUM THIOPENTAL
(LETHAL DOSE—SEDATES PERSON)

PANCURONIUM BROMIDE
(MUSCLE RELAXANT—COLLAPSES DIAPHRAM AND LUNGS)

POTASSIUM CHLORIDE
(STOPS HEART)

OFFENDER IS USUALLY PRONOUNCED
DEAD APPROXIMATELY
7-11 MINUTES AFTER
THE PROCESS BEGINS.

 The cost of drugs per
execution is $1,287 in Texas

IN THE CASE OF AN UNORTHODOX OR UNAVAILABLE LAST MEAL REQUEST, THE MOST READILY AVAILABLE SUBSTITUTE WILL BE MADE

MOST STATES SERVE THE MEAL A DAY OR TWO PRIOR TO EXECUTION AND USE THE EUPHEMISM, "SPECIAL MEAL"

THE RULES FOR LAST MEALS IN THE USA

IN THE STATE OF GEORGIA, THE TOTAL COST OF THE LAST MEAL MUST BE UNDER $20$20$20

MOST STATES DO NOT **ALLOW THOSE** ON DEATH ROW TO REQUEST **ALCOHOL OR TOBACCO**

Death By Numbers

American states with the death penalty in place 32

American states with NO death penalty in place 18

American states that have recently abolished the death penalty:

Maryland, May 2013
Connecticut, April 2012
New Mexico, March 2009

Number of executions by method in the USA since 1976

(as of April 2014)

Lethal injection 1199

Electrocution 158

Gas chamber 111

Hanging 3

Firing squad 3

10 Most Deadly States in the USA

(Based on the number of executions since 1976)

Texas	Florida	Georgia
513	85	53
Virginia	Missouri	Ohio
110	73	53
Oklahoma	Alabama	North Carolina
110	56	43

"But I didn't do it!"

Since 1973, over **140** people have been released from death row based on evidence to support their innocence.

THE MOST FREQUENTLY REQUESTED LAST MEALS BY DEATH ROW PRISONERS

This shows the most popular last meals of USA prisoners and was compiled using data from the State Of Texas Penitentiary.

TOP 8 IN ORDER OF POPULARITY

1
CHEESEBURGER

2
STEAK

3
FRIED CHICKEN

4
EGGS:
SCRAMBLED OR FRIED/OMELETS ALONG WITH OTHER BREAKFAST ITEMS

5
FRIED CHICKEN STEAK

6
EGGS:
WITH ACCOMPANYING MEXICAN SIDE DISHES, e.g. BEANS AND RICE, SALSA, etc.

7
PLAIN BURGER

8
LIVER AND ONION

ROGUES' GALLERY:
DEAD MEN WALKING

Lawrence Russell Brewer
(1967–2011)

CRIME: Brewer was convicted, along with accomplices Shawn Berry and John King, of the cruel murder of James Byrd, Jr. who was dragged along behind a truck. Brewer refused to eat his final meal with the result that no one else is allowed this privilege in Texas today.

EXECUTION: Huntsville Unit, Texas, September 21, 2011, by lethal injection

ON THE MENU: Fried chicken steaks with onions and gravy, a triple cheeseburger, a large meat and vegetable omelet, fried okra with loads of ketchup, loaf of bread, 1 pound of barbecued meat, a meat feast pizza, 3 fajitas, 2 cans of soda, and, to round it all off, some peanut-butter fudge and a pint of ice cream!

Timothy McVeigh

(1968–2001)

CRiME: Gulf War veteran and American terrorist Timothy McVeigh was responsible for the deaths of 168 men, women, and children on April 19, 1995, in the Oklahoma City bombing. Over 680 other people were injured in the attack. McVeigh apparently perpetrated the terrorist attack in response to the Waco siege of 1993, in which 76 people died. McVeigh asked for his execution to be televised. His request was denied.

EXECUTION: US Federal Penitentiary, Terre Haute, Indiana, June 11, 2001, by lethal injection

ON THE MENU: 2 pints of mint chocolate chip ice cream

Mark Dean Schwab

(1968–2008)

CRiME: Convicted on May 22, 1992, Schwab was sentenced to death for the kidnap, assault, and murder of Junny Rios-Martinez, Jr., an 11-year-old boy from Cocoa, Florida. Lengthy appeals and stays of execution meant he was not executed for his crimes for 16 years.

EXECUTiON: Florida State Prison, July 1, 2008, by lethal injection

ON THE MENU: Bacon, sausage, fried eggs, hash browns, buttered toast, and a glass of chocolate milk

Lawrence Russell Brewer was the very last prisoner to receive a last-meal request in the State of Texas!

Miguel Richardson (1954–2001)

CRIME: Richardson was convicted in 1981 of the murders of security guards John Ebbert and Howard Powers, while escaping after a robbery at the Holiday Inn in San Antonio, Texas.

EXECUTION: Huntsville Unit, Texas, June 26, 2001, by lethal injection

ON THE MENU: 1 chef's salad (with Thousand Island dressing), 1 coconut, 1 kiwi juice, 1 pineapple juice, 1 mango, some grapes, some lettuce, cottage cheese, 2 peaches, 1 banana, 1 apple, 1 fruit salad, some cheese, and 1 sliced tomato

PLUS A chocolate birthday cake with the date of his wedding anniversary—2/23/90—on top and 7 pink candles!

Odell Barnes, Jr.
(1968–2000)

CRIME: Construction worker Odell Barnes, from Wichita County, Texas, was found guilty of the 1989 murder of Helen Bass, who returned home and found him robbing her home.

EXECUTION: Huntsville Unit, Texas, March 1, 2000, by lethal injection

ON THE MENU: Rather than requesting a last meal, Odell Barnes called instead for "Justice, equality, and world peace."

Gary Michael Heidnik
(1943–1999)

CRIME: In 1986 and 1987, Heidnik held six women prisoner in his Philadelphia home, where he tortured and brutalized them. Four of the women survived, but Heidnik was sentenced to death for murdering the other two women, Sandra Lindsay and Deborah Dudley.

EXECUTION: Rockview State Correctional Institution, Pennsylvania, July 6, 1999, by lethal injection

ON THE MENU: 2 slices of cheese pizza and 2 cups of coffee

Stranger than fiction!

Author Thomas Harris drew on the Heidnik story as inspiration for one of the characters, Buffalo Bill, in his book Silence of the Lambs.

Walter Le Grand
(1962–1999)

CRIME:

On January 7, 1982, Walter Le Grand and his brother, Karl, murdered bank manager Ken Hartsock during a failed robbery at the Valley National Bank in Marana, Arizona.

EXECUTION:

Pima County, Arizona, March 3, 1999, in the gas chamber

ON THE MENU:
6 eggs-over-easy, 16 pieces of bacon, hash browns, 1 breakfast steak, some hot sauce, 1 pint of pineapple sherbet ice cream, 3 different cans of soda, and 1 cup of coffee with 2 packs of sugar.

PLUS: 4 Rolaid tablets!

Robert Madden
(1963–1997)

CRIME:

Madden was condemned to die for stabbing Herbert Elvin Megason and his son, Gary Lynn Megason, to death on September 15, 1985.

EXECUTION:

Huntsville Unit, Texas, May 28, 1997, by lethal injection

ON THE MENU: Asked for his final meal to be given to a homeless person. Request was denied.

Delbert Teague, Jr.
(1962–1998)

CRIME:

On April 28, 1985, construction worker Teague shot Kevin Leroy Allen, in Texas, before abducting Donna Irwin.

EXECUTION:

Huntsville Unit, Texas, September 9, 1998, by lethal injection

ON THE MENU: A cheeseburger, (his Mom told him to—he'd apparently wanted nothing to eat at all)

Thomas Grasso
(1960–1995)

CRiME: Grasso was found guilty of double murder, first strangling 87-year-old Hilda Johnson with Christmas tree lights, and then 81-year-old Leslie Holtz in New York six months later.

EXECUTION: Oklahoma State Penitentiary, March 20, 1995, by lethal injection

ON THE MENU: Double Burger King cheeseburger, a can of spaghetti and meatballs, 24 steamed mussels, 24 steamed clams with a wedge of lemon, 6 barbecued spare ribs, pumpkin pie with whipped cream, some strawberries, 2 strawberry milkshakes

Ted Bundy
(1946–1989)

CRiME: This American serial killer assaulted and murdered many young women during the 1970s and earlier. He later confessed to over 30 murders.

EXECUTION: Florida State Prison, January 24, 1989, by electrocution

ON THE MENU: Bundy was offered—but refused to eat—the traditional medium-rare steak, eggs-over-easy, hash browns, toast with butter and jelly, milk, coffee, juice

Ricky Ray Rector
(1950–1992)

CRIME: Convicted for the 1981 murder of Arthur Criswell and Robert Martin, Rector spent a decade on death row before his execution. He shot his first victim at a nightclub in Conway, Arkansas. Although Rector had decided to hand himself in, he also shot Officer Robert Martin when he arrived at the scene. On trying—and failing—to commit suicide, Rector suffered horrific brain damage.

EXECUTION: Cummins Unit, Arkansas, January 24, 1992, by lethal injection

> **ON THE MENU:** Steak, fried chicken, cherry-flavored Kool-Aid, and a slice of pecan pie

Strange but true!

Clearly, Rector was not quite himself. So badly had his brain been damaged in his bungled suicide attempt that he did not eat the pecan pie, believing he could save it for later.

James Edward Smith
(1952–1990)

CRIME: Found guilty of murdering Larry D. Rohus, an insurance executive, on March 7, 1983, Smith became famous for his very strange last-supper request—he asked for a lump of dirt, perhaps for use in a voodoo ritual.

EXECUTION: Huntsville Unit, Texas, June 26, 1990, by lethal injection

> **ON THE MENU:** A lump of dirt—instead, prison staff gave him yogurt.

ROGUES' GALLERY:
DEAD WOMEN WALKING

As of April 1, 2013, there were 63 women awaiting execution on Death Row. Fourteen women have been put to death in the United States since 1976. Here are some of their stories and last-supper requests:

Kimberley McCarthy
(1961–2013)

CRIME: Sentenced to death for murdering her neighbor, Dorothy Booth, during a robbery in 1997.

EXECUTION: Huntsville Unit, Texas, June 26, 2013, by a single lethal injection of pentobarbital

ON THE MENU: Texas abolished the right of inmates to request a last meal in 2011. However, McCarthy's last known meal was pepper steak, mashed potatoes and gravy, mixed vegetables, and white cake with chocolate icing.

Aileen Wuornos

(1956–2002)

CRIME: Serial killer Wuornos was convicted of murdering six men in Florida between 1989 and 1990.

EXECUTION: Florida State Prison, October 9, 2002, by lethal injection

ON THE MENU: Cup of coffee

Teresa Lewis

(1969–2010)

CRIME: Although not directly involved, Lewis was sentenced to death for masterminding the murder of her husband and stepson, Julian and Charles Lewis, in an attempt to claim on an insurance policy.

EXECUTION: Greensville Correctional Center, Virginia, September 23, 2010, by lethal injection

The first woman to be executed by the State of Virginia since 17-year-old Virginia Christian in 1912.

ON THE MENU: Fried chicken, sweet peas with butter, German chocolate cake, and a Dr Pepper.

Karla Faye Tucker

(1959–1998)

CRIME: On June 13, 1983, Tucker used a pickaxe to kill Jerry Lynn Dean and Deborah Thornton, while attempting to steal a motorbike with her boyfriend, Danny Garrett.

EXECUTION: Huntsville Unit, Texas, February 3, 1998, by lethal injection

ON THE MENU: Banana, peach, and garden salad with a ranch dressing

Judy Buenoano

(1943–1998)

CRIME: Often referred to as the "Black Widow," Buenoano was sentenced to death on November 16, 1985, for poisoning her husband, James Goodyear, with arsenic.

EXECUTION: Florida State Prison, March 30, 1998, by electrocution

> **ON THE MENU:**
> Broccoli, tomato, and asparagus salad, strawberries, and a cup of tea

Judy was the first woman executed in the State of Florida since 1848.

Velma Barfield

(1932–1984)

CRIME: Barfield was convicted of the murder of her boyfriend, Stuart Taylor, on December 2, 1978, using a concoction of beer and arsenic. Although only convicted of one murder, she later confessed to killing six other people.

EXECUTION: North Carolina Central Prison, November 2, 1984, by lethal injection

> **ON THE MENU:** Bag of Cheeze Doodles and a coke

Known as the "Death Row Granny," Velma was the first woman to be executed in the USA since the reintroduction of the death penalty in 1976.

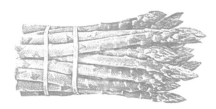

INFAMOUS AMERICAN PARTNERS-IN-CRIME!

Perry Edward Smith
(1928–1965)

Richard Eugene Hickock
(1931–1965)

CRIME: Executed for the brutal murders of four members of the Clutter family in Holcomb, Kansas, on November 15, 1959.

EXECUTION: Lansing Correctional Facility, Kansas, April 14, 1965, by hanging

❖ ❖ ❖ ❖ ❖ ❖ ❖ ❖ ❖ ❖ ❖

ON THE MENU: Partners to the end, Smith and Hickock had the same last meal— shrimp, French fries, garlic bread, ice cream, strawberries and whipped cream

Stranger than fiction!

Author Truman Capote made Smith and Hickock's crime famous in his book In Cold Blood (1966).

Eva Coo
(1889–1935)

CRIME: Born in Canada, brothel keeper Eva Coo was convicted of murdering Henry Wright on June 14, 1934, in an attempt to collect his life insurance money.

EXECUTION: Sing Sing Correctional Facility, New York State, June 27, 1935, by electrocution

ON THE MENU: Piece of toast, ice cream, and a cup of tea

❖ ❖ ❖ ❖ ❖ ❖ ❖ ❖ ❖ ❖ ❖ ❖ ❖ ❖ ❖

Anne Marie Hahn
(1906–1938)

The first woman to die of electrocution in Ohio!

CRIME: German-born female serial killer who poisoned six elderly men for whom she worked as a live-in nurse.

EXECUTION: Ohio Penitentiary, December 7, 1938, by electrocution

ON THE MENU: Cake and punch, which Hahn supposedly offered to members of the press who visited her cell just before she was executed.

IN EUROPE

Edith Thompson
(1893–1923)

CRiME: Thompson was found guilty of conspiring to murder her husband, Percy Thompson, after a trip to a London theater on October 3, 1922. As they returned home, Percy was fatally stabbed by Edith's lover, Frederick Bywaters. Edith later claimed to have been unaware of Frederick's plans, but both were sentenced to hang.

EXECUTION: HM Prison Holloway, London, January 9, 1923, by hanging

ON THE MENU:
Toast and an apple

Ruth Ellis
(1926–1955)

The last woman to be hanged in the United Kingdom

CRiME: A model and London nightclub hostess, Ellis was convicted of murdering her lover, David Blakely, in the street. Their stormy relationship led to a fatal shooting outside the Magdala pub in Hampstead, London.

EXECUTION: HM Prison Holloway, London, July 13, 1955, by hanging

ON THE MENU:
A large brandy

Ruth Ellis' words on being arrested:
"I am guilty, I'm a little confused."

Peter Kürten
(1883–1931)

CRIME: Known as the "Vampire of Düsseldorf," Kürten was a German serial killer who was most active in 1929.

EXECUTION: Cologne, Germany, July 2, 1931, decapitation by guillotine

ON THE MENU: Wiener schnitzel, fried potatoes, and a bottle of white wine. He asked for seconds—and received them.

Higinia Balaguer
(Died 1890)

CRIME: Balaguer was a Spanish maid who, along with accomplice Dolores Avila, was found guilty of robbery and murder. Dolores was imprisoned for 18 years, but Higinia received the death sentence.

EXECUTION: Killed by garrote (strangulation) while tied to a wooden post, in Madrid, Spain, on June 19, 1890

ON THE MENU: Vermicelli soup, hake, and cherries in syrup

> "THERE ARE PEOPLE IN THE WORLD
> SO HUNGRY THAT GOD CANNOT
> APPEAR TO THEM EXCEPT IN
> THE FORM OF BREAD."
>
> MAHATMA GANDHI
> (1869-1948)

WORLD LEADERS

& POLITICAL FIGURES

❦ ❦ ❦ ❦ ❦ ❦ ❦ ❦ ❦ ❦ ❦ ❦ ❦ ❦

THESE PEOPLE HAVE ALL DOMINATED THE
WORLD STAGE AT SOME POINT IN HISTORY
AND LEFT A LASTING POLITICAL,
CULTURAL, OR RELIGIOUS LEGACY. BUT
WHAT WERE THEIR LAST WORDS AND, MORE
IMPORTANTLY, THEIR LAST MEALS?

❦ ❦ ❦ ❦ ❦ ❦ ❦ ❦ ❦ ❦ ❦ ❦ ❦ ❦

POLITICAL FOOD FACTS

TOP TIPPLES OF FAMOUS WORLD LEADERS

NAPOLEON BONAPARTE (1769–1821)
CHAMBERTIN RED WINE (FROM BURGUNDY)

WINSTON CHURCHILL (1874–1965)
CHAMPAGNE, SCOTCH, BRANDY, MARTINI

3RD US PRESIDENT THOMAS JEFFERSON (1743–1826)
WINE

33RD US PRESIDENT HARRY S. TRUMAN (1884–1972)
BOURBON

37TH US PRESIDENT RICHARD NIXON (1913–1994)
RUM AND COKE, MARTINI

38TH US PRESIDENT GERALD FORD (1913–2006)
GIN AND TONIC

ADOLF HITLER
1889–1945

German dictator and leader of the Nazi Party, Hitler took his life when he realized that World War Two was over. On April 29, 1945, while hiding in his bunker in Berlin, Hitler married his girlfriend, Eva Braun. At 15:30 on April 30, Hitler and Eva ended their lives.

CAUSE OF DEATH

Hitler: Suicide by gun-shot to right temple

Braun: Suicide by cyanide pill

ON THE MENU
Spaghetti with a simple sauce

HERMANN WILHELM GÖRING

1893–1946

A German politician, military leader, and leading member of the Nazi Party

GÖRING WAS FOUND GUILTY OF CRIMES AGAINST HUMANITY AT THE FIRST NUREMBERG TRIAL OF 1945-1946. HE ASKED TO BE SHOT LIKE A SOLDIER, BUT HIS REQUEST WAS DENIED AND HE WAS CONDEMNED TO HANG. GÖRING KILLED HIMSELF BEFORE THE DEATH SENTENCE COULD BE CARRIED OUT.

ON THE MENU POTASSIUM CYANIDE CAPSULE
CAUSE OF DEATH SUICIDE

SADDAM HUSSEIN

1937–2006

Infamous Iraqi dictator Saddam Hussein was sentenced to death for crimes against humanity. President of Iraq from 1979 to 2003, until he was overthrown following an invasion by coalition forces, he was executed on Saturday, December 30, 2006.

CAUSE OF DEATH

HANGING

ON THE MENU

BOILED
CHICKEN
WITH RICE
CUPS OF HOT
WATER WITH
HONEY

Some Untimely Demises of UNITED STATES Presidents

ZACHARY TAYLOR

1784–1850

12TH PRESIDENT OF THE UNITED STATES

WHILE ATTENDING THE JULY 4TH CELEBRATIONS AT THE WASHINGTON MONUMENT ON A VERY HOT DAY, TAYLOR WAS TAKEN SERIOUSLY ILL WITH SEVERE ABDOMINAL PAINS AND NAUSEA. HE DIED FIVE DAYS LATER.

On the menu

LOTS OF CHERRIES AND GLASSES OF ICED MILK AND WATER

Cause of death

POSSIBLY *CHOLERA MORBUS* (OR GASTROENTERITIS), AS A RESULT OF SOMETHING HE'D EATEN

ABRAHAM LINCOLN

THE 16TH PRESIDENT OF THE UNITED STATES OF AMERICA

Mock turtle soup, roast Virginia fowl with chestnut
stuffing and baked yams, cauliflower with cheese sauce

On April 14, 1865, President Lincoln was
assassinated by John Wilkes Booth—an actor angry
about Lincoln's anti-slavery beliefs and involvement
in the American Civil War—while he attended a
performance of *Our American Cousin* at Ford's Theater.
As Lincoln sat in his box, Booth crept up behind him
and shot him in the head.

CAUSE OF DEATH
Shot in the head at point-blank range

THERE HAVE BEEN MULTIPLE ASSASSINATION ATTEMPTS AND PLOTS ON PRESIDENTS OF THE UNITED STATES.

OF THESE, FOUR HAVE BEEN SUCCESSFUL—NAMELY PRESIDENTS ABRAHAM LINCOLN, JAMES GARFIELD, WILLIAM MCKINLEY, AND JOHN F. KENNEDY.

FRANKLIN
DELANO ROOSEVELT

1882-1945

THE 32ND PRESIDENT OF THE UNITED STATES OF AMERICA

HE DIED A FEW MONTHS BEFORE THE JAPANESE SURRENDER

ON THE MENU

Breakfast in bed: fried eggs, bacon, one slice of toast

CAUSE OF DEATH
Stroke

John F. Kennedy

THE 35ᵀᴴ PRESIDENT OF THE UNITED STATES OF AMERICA

1917– 1963

Kennedy spoke to supporters at a breakfast meeting just prior to his ill-fated parade in Dallas, Texas.

On the menu

Soft-boiled eggs
Bacon
Toast with marmalade
Orange juice
Coffee

Cause of death

Assassinated by gun shots to the head and throat

Last words: "That's obvious."

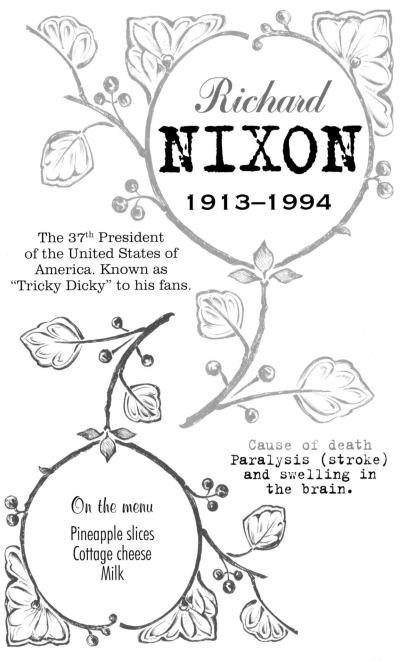

Richard
NIXON
1913–1994

The 37th President of the United States of America. Known as "Tricky Dicky" to his fans.

Cause of death
Paralysis (stroke) and swelling in the brain.

On the menu
Pineapple slices
Cottage cheese
Milk

Activists and Political Figures

Martin Luther King, Jr.

1929   **1968**

American religious leader,
political rights activist, and
peace-loving humanitarian, King was
assassinated by James
Earl Ray on Thursday, April 4, 1968,
on a balcony of the Lorraine Motel
in Memphis, Tennessee.
He was 39 years old.

ON THE MENU

Southern fried chicken
with Louisiana hot sauce, black-eyed peas,
collard greens, and corn bread

CAUSE OF DEATH Shot dead with a single bullet

MAHATMA GANDHI
1869-1948

On January 30, 1948, spiritual leader Gandhi took an evening walk at Birla Bhavan, in New Delhi, India. Although he often met and greeted followers on these walks, on this fateful night he met an assassin who shot him at point-blank range.

CAUSE OF DEATH
Fatal shooting

ON THE MENU
Goat's milk
Cooked vegetables
Oranges and a concoction of ginger, sour lemons, and strained butter with aloe vera juice

469–399BC

Socrates

On the menu: Hemlock-laced drink

Cause of death: Hemlock poisoning

The classical Greek philosopher Socrates
was tried and condemned to die in Athens,
Greece, by consuming a drink containing
hemlock, which is poisonous.

*"Worthless people live only to eat
and drink; people of worth
eat and drink only to live."*
(Socrates)

President of France from 1981 to 1995, Mitterand died on January 8, 1996, just eight months after leaving office.

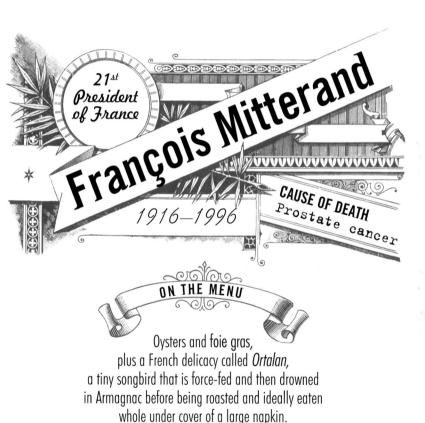

François Mitterand

21st President of France

1916–1996

CAUSE OF DEATH
Prostate cancer

ON THE MENU

Oysters and foie gras,
plus a French delicacy called *Ortolan*,
a tiny songbird that is force-fed and then drowned
in Armagnac before being roasted and ideally eaten
whole under cover of a large napkin.

The practice is now illegal.

THE LAST SUPPER—THIS IS PERHAPS THE MOST FAMOUS AND FREQUENTLY ILLUSTRATED OF ALL LAST MEALS.

ACCORDING TO CHRISTIAN DOCTRINE, THE LAST SUPPER IS THE FINAL MEAL THAT JESUS SHARED WITH THE APOSTLES IN JERUSALEM BEFORE HE WAS CRUCIFIED.

ACCORDING TO BIBLICAL ACCOUNTS, JESUS SENT TWO OF HIS DISCIPLES TO PREPARE THE MEAL AND GATHERED ALL THE DISCIPLES IN A ROOM. HE THEN FORETOLD THAT ONE OF THE DISCIPLES WOULD BETRAY HIM—THIS PERSON WAS JUDAS ISCARIOT.

AFTER BLESSING SOME BREAD AND WINE AND GIVING THESE TO THE DISCIPLES TO EAT AND DRINK, JESUS EXPLAINED THAT THE BREAD REPRESENTED HIS BODY AND THE WINE SYMBOLIZED HIS BLOOD.

JESUS CHRIST

On the menu
Bread and Wine

Cause of death
Crucifixion

"YOUR CLOTHES SHOULD BE TIGHT
ENOUGH TO SHOW YOU'RE A WOMAN,
BUT LOOSE ENOUGH TO SHOW
YOU'RE A LADY."

MARILYN MONROE
(1926–1962)

FILM STARS

& OTHER CELEBRITIES

❧ ❧ ❧ ❧ ❧ ❧ ❧ ❧ ❧ ❧ ❧ ❧ ❧ ❧ ❧

CELEBRITIES MAKE UP THE FUN FABRIC OF OUR
DAILY LIVES: IN SONG, FILM, IN THE NEWS,
AND IN THE GOSSIP COLUMNS. THESE CELEBRITIES
HAVE ALL BECOME FAMOUS (AND INFAMOUS) IN
THEIR OWN RIGHT, AS SINGERS, SONGWRITERS,
ACTORS, AND ENTERTAINERS, BUT WHAT WERE
THEIR LAST MEALS?

❧ ❧ ❧ ❧ ❧ ❧ ❧ ❧ ❧ ❧ ❧ ❧ ❧ ❧ ❧

CELEB FOOD FACTS

ACTORS WHO DIED WHILE FILMING A MOVIE

OLIVER REED (1938–1999)
Died from a heart attack drinking in The Pub in Valletta, Malta, while filming *Gladiator*. Reed's favorite drink at the pub was Löwenbräu lager.

RIVER PHOENIX (1970–1993)
Young and promising American actor who died from heart failure (possibly drug-induced) on Hallowe'en morning outside The Viper Room on Sunset Strip, Hollywood, while filming *Dark Blood*. River was known as "the vegan James Dean."

HEATH LEDGER (1979–2008)
Australian actor who died at home after an accidental overdose of prescription pills during the filming of *The Imaginarium of Doctor Parnassus*.

POPULAR FILM-STAR RESTAURANTS

ROMANOFF'S
Beverley Hills, California, a favorite with Humphrey Bogart—Bogie often ordered ham and eggs.

BUFFET DE LA GARE DE CELIGNY
A French restaurant in Geneva, Switzerland, loved by Richard Burton.

MORTON'S
A steak house in Chicago, Illinois, visited by "Ol' Blue Eyes"—Frank Sinatra.

CHASEN'S
in West Hollywood, California, a favorite of Alfred Hitchcock, Bob Hope, Gregory Peck, and Kirk Douglas. Later years saw Mel Gibson, Warren Beatty, and Jack Nicholson become regulars.

MEALS MOVIE STARS LOVED TO MAKE!

ELIZABETH TAYLOR
(1932–2011)
Chicken with avocado and mushrooms

PATRICK SWAYZE
(1952–2009)
Chicken pie

FRANK SINATRA (1915–1998)
Barbecued lamb

KATHERINE HEPBURN
(1907–2003)
Chocolate brownies

JUDY GARLAND
(1922–1969)
Steak and kidney pie

JAMES DEAN

1931-1955

❊ ❊ ❊ ❊ ❊ ❊ ❊ ❊ ❊ ❊ ❊ ❊ ❊ ❊

Young actor and American rebel James Dean
made a huge impact in a very short time
with three iconic films:
Rebel Without a Cause (1955),
East of Eden (1955),
and *Giant* (1956).

On September 30, 1955, while on his way to a car rally in Salinas, California, with his car mechanic, Rolf Wütheric, Dean crashed his Porsche 550 Spyder. En route, Dean had stopped at a roadside diner for a bite to eat.

This was to be the last refreshment he ever took. Traveling on Highway 466, Dean hit another car head-on. His companion survived the car crash. Dean was just 24 years old.

ON THE MENU
Apple pie
Glass of milk

CAUSE OF DEATH
Car crash

JOHN BELUSHI

1949–1982

American actor John Belushi visited the
Rainbow Bar and Grill, in Los Angeles,
on March 5, 1982, where he ate before
returning with his girlfriend to the
Chateau Marmont Hotel on
Sunset Boulevard.

ON THE MENU

Lentil soup

CAUSE OF DEATH
Lethal overdose of
cocaine and heroine

MARLENE DIETRICH

1901-1992

ON THE MENU
A FEW SPOONFULS OF SOUP

Originally from Berlin, Germany, Marie Magdalene Dietrich was an actress and singer who enjoyed a long and varied career. Some of her best-known roles include Lola Lola in *The Blue Angel* (1930) and Shanghai Lily in *Shanghai Express* (1932).

After suffering a stroke in 1992, she lost her appetite, but managed a few spoonfuls of soup before dying peacefully at the age of 90.

CAUSE OF DEATH
STROKE

OLIVE THOMAS
1894–1920

American silent movie actress and model whose films included *The Glorious Lady* (1919) and *The Flapper* (1920). Married to actor John Pickford, Olive died after accidentally ingesting a topical medicine prescribed to treat her husband's syphilis-related sores.

CAUSE OF DEATH
POISONING BY MISADVENTURE

ON THE MENU

Lethal dose of
mercury bichloride

JAMES GANDOLFINI

1961–2013

An American actor who won acclaim for his role as Tony Soprano in the cult series, *The Sopranos*, James Gandolfini was found dead in his bathroom at the hotel *Boscolo Exedra*, on June 19, 2013, in Rome.

ON THE MENU
FRIED PRAWNS, SOME FOIE GRAS, AND VARIOUS ALCOHOLIC DRINKS

CAUSE OF DEATH
HEART ATTACK

John Candy

American comedy actor John Candy died in Durango, Mexico, while filming his latest movie, *Wagons East!* He was perhaps most famous for *Planes, Trains, and Automobiles (1987)*.

He died March 4, 1994.

On the menu
Pasta meal to celebrate a good day's filming

Cause of death
Heart attack

1950–1994

> *"I should never have switched from Scotch to Martinis."*
> (Humphrey Bogart, 1899–1957)

Brittany Murphy 1977–2009

An American movie and stage actress, as well as a singer, Murphy was born in Atlanta before moving to Los Angeles to pursue her career as an actress. She died at the age of 32.

On the menu

Some noodles, Thai food,
a Gatorade, water, and tea with lemon

Cause of death

Cardiac arrest after collapsing in the bathroom

> *"I never worry about diets. The only carrots that interest me are the number you get in a diamond."*
> (Mae West, 1893–1980)

Marilyn MONROE

1926-1962

BORN
Norma Jeane Mortensen
BAPTIZED
Norma Jeane Baker

Marilyn's home:

The words *Cursum perficio*—meaning "My journey ends here"—are inscribed in the tiles at the entrance to the last home she ever bought.

Cause of death

A POSSIBLE OVERDOSE OF BARBITURATES

THE FINAL YEARS OF MARILYN'S LIFE WERE MARKED BY ILLNESS, PERSONAL PROBLEMS, AND A REPUTATION FOR BEING UNRELIABLE AND DIFFICULT TO WORK WITH. HER DEATH HAS BEEN THE SUBJECT OF A GREAT DEAL OF CONTROVERSY. THOUGH OFFICIALLY CLASSIFIED AS A "PROBABLE SUICIDE," THE POSSIBILITIES OF ACCIDENTAL OVERDOSE OR HOMICIDE HAVE NEVER BEEN RULED OUT.

Marilyn Monroe was an iconic American actress, singer, and model. Some of her most celebrated films include *Gentlemen Prefer Blondes* (1953), *The Seven Year Itch* (1955), and *Some Like It Hot* (1959). Marilyn was found dead in the bedroom of her Brentwood home, in Los Angeles, on August 5, 1962. She was only 36 years old. She is buried at Westwood Memorial Park, in Los Angeles. Baseball star Joe DiMaggio, to whom Marilyn was married for just nine months in 1954, sent red roses weekly to her grave for 20 years.

On the menu

Mexican buffet selection and champagne

Two of Marilyn's favorite restaurants

Villa Nova (now the *Rainbow Bar and Grill*) on Sunset Boulevard, in West Hollywood, where Marilyn Monroe and Joe DiMaggio met on a blind date in 1953

Formosa Café, Santa Monica Boulevard, West Hollywood

James Stewart

Famous for his distinctive voice, James Stewart, from Pennsylvania, was a much-loved American film and stage actor. He is perhaps best known for the 1946 film *It's A Wonderful Life*.

James Stewart conducted regular telephone interviews with the *National Enquirer* magazine. On Wednesday 2nd July, 1997—the day he died—Stewart gave the magazine details of that day's meals.

ON THE MENU

Lunch
Peanut butter and jelly

....

Dinner
Corned game hen and carrots

....

CAUSE OF DEATH
Pulmonary embolism

1908–1997

MITSUGORO BANDO VIII

1906–1975

ON THE MENU

FOUR FUGU FISH

CAUSE OF DEATH

**ACUTE POISONING LEADING
TO PARALYSIS AND DEATH**

The acclaimed Japanese actor Mitsugoro Bando VIII died on January 16, 1975, after eating some **fugu fish** (also known as puffer fish). The internal organs, especially the liver, of fugu fish contain a deadly neurotoxin called tetrodotoxin, which is **over a thousand times deadlier than cyanide**.

In Japan, highly trained chefs prepare these fish by removing all of the internal organs. For this reason the fish is regarded as a culinary delicacy that only the very brave (or very foolhardy) are tempted to eat.

It is like playing a game of gastronomic Russian roulette. There is no known antidote.

1946– GIOVANNI –1997 VERSACE

Italian fashion designer and founder of the fashion house *Versace*, Giovanni Versace was also renowned for the costumes he designed for film and theater, as well as for his circle of famous friends, which included Diana, Princess of Wales, Eric Clapton, Madonna, and Sting. On the morning of July 15, 1997, Versace was shot dead by Andrew Cunanan outside his mansion in Miami Beach, Florida. Cunanan used the same gun to shoot himself days later.

CAUSE OF DEATH
Fatal shooting

ON THE MENU
Two eggs-over-easy, bacon, some wholewheat toast, and black coffee

Lou Costello

1906–1959

American film actor and comedian Lou Costello was famous as one half of the comic duo, Abbot and Costello. Hilarious films they made together include *Buck Privates* (1941), *In The Navy* (1941), and *Keep 'Em Flying* (1941). Costello died at Doctors' Hospital in Beverley Hills, Los Angeles, on March 3, 1959.

On the menu **Strawberry ice cream soda**

Cause of death **Heart attack**

Sócrates

1954–2011

World-famous Brazilian footballer Sócrates died on December 4, 2011, in São Paulo, Brazil, after being taken seriously ill with food poisoning, which was probably made worse by alcohol abuse. His wife and friend were also taken ill after the meal, but survived.

ON THE MENU
BEEF STROGANOFF

CAUSE OF DEATH
INTESTINAL INFECTION LEADING TO SEPTIC SHOCK

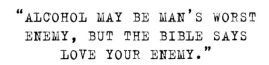

"ALCOHOL MAY BE MAN'S WORST
ENEMY, BUT THE BIBLE SAYS
LOVE YOUR ENEMY."

FRANK SINATRA
(1915-1998)

ROCK STARS

& MUSICIANS

⚜ ⚜ ⚜ ⚜ ⚜ ⚜ ⚜ ⚜ ⚜ ⚜ ⚜ ⚜ ⚜ ⚜

ALTHOUGH SOME OF THESE MUSICIANS LIVED LIFE ON THE EDGE, PLAYING AND PARTYING HARD, MANY MADE SURPRISING MEAL CHOICES— FROM MICHAEL JACKSON'S HEALTHY TUNA SUPPER TO FRANK SINATRA'S GRILLED CHEESE COMFORT FOOD. DISCOVER HOW THESE ICONS OF MUSIC LIVED AND DIED—AND WHETHER THEIR LAST MEAL PLAYED A PART IN THEIR DEMISE.

⚜ ⚜ ⚜ ⚜ ⚜ ⚜ ⚜ ⚜ ⚜ ⚜ ⚜ ⚜ ⚜ ⚜

ROCK-STAR FACTS

ROCK STARS WHO DRANK— PROBABLY TO THE DEATH!

JANIS JOPLIN (1943–1970)
Loved Southern Comfort, although
a heroin overdose killed her in 1970.

JOHN BONHAM, LED ZEPPELIN'S DRUMMER (1948–1980)
Regularly downed large quantities of vodka,
eventually choking on his own vomit after
a vodka binge in 1980.

BON SCOTT, AC/DC'S LEAD SINGER (1946–1980)
Partial to a drink or two, Scott died after
a night of binge drinking in 1980.

GENE VINCENT (1935–1971)
American rockabilly singer whose
alcohol dependency probably led to
a heart attack in 1971.

Wolfgang Amadeus Mozart

1756 — 1791

A child musical prodigy who became one of the most famous classical composers in the world. Although rumors abound that he was murdered by his arch-rival Salieri, he probably died from a fatal disease called trichinosis after eating undercooked pork chops.

ON THE MENU

Pork chops that were probably undercooked

CAUSE OF DEATH:
Trichinosis
(a parasitic disease)

"The taste of death is upon my lips. I feel something that is not of this earth."

(Mozart's dying words)

JOHN LENNON

1940- -1980

Talented song writer and musician John Lennon was one of the Fab Four—aka *The Beatles*—a band from Liverpool that was perhaps the most influential pop group of the twentieth century. On December 8, 1980, as Lennon arrived at his apartment in the Dakota Building, near Central Park in New York, with his wife, Yoko Ono, he was shot by a fan, Mark David Chapman.

CAUSE OF DEATH Shot in the back

ON THE MENU

Corned beef sandwich

"We're trying to sell peace, like a product, you know, and sell it like people sell soap or soft drinks."

John Lennon
(The David Frost Show, 1969)

FRANK SINATRA

1915–1998

Legendary singer and actor Frank Sinatra, originally from New Jersey, enjoyed a stratospheric career in showbusiness, lasting for over 60 years. He died on May 14, 1998, in Los Angeles, California.

ON THE MENU

Grilled cheese sandwich

CAUSE OF DEATH:
Heart attack

Last words: "I'm losing."

One of Frank's favorite restaurants was *Patsy's* Italian restaurant in Manhattan, New York City.

ELVIS PRESLEY

THE KING OF ROCK 'N' ROLL

1935-1977

ON THE MENU

**4 SCOOPS
OF ICE CREAM
6 CHOCOLATE
CHIP COOKIES**

BORN ELVIS AARON PRESLEY IN TUPELO, MISSISSIPPI, ELVIS WAS AN ICONIC AMERICAN SINGER AND ACTOR. HE DIED ALONE IN TRAGIC CIRCUMSTANCES IN THE BATHROOM OF HIS GRACELAND HOME AT THE AGE OF ONLY 42.

CAUSE OF DEATH

Cardiac arrhythmia
(or irregular beating
of the heart)

DOCTORS BELIEVE THAT ELVIS' HEART IRREGULARITY MAY HAVE BEEN CAUSED BY AN OVERDOSE OF PRESCRIPTION DRUGS (INCLUDING CODEINE, MORPHINE, AND VALIUM). NO ONE WILL KNOW FOR CERTAIN JUST YET, THOUGH, AS ELVIS' FATHER, VERNON PRESLEY, HAS ENSURED THAT THE FULL AUTOPSY REPORT WILL REMAIN SEALED UNTIL 2027.

What happened on that fateful night August 16, 1977?

Elvis and his girlfriend, Ginger Alden, returned to Graceland at midnight following a trip to the dentist. After an early-hours'session of racquetball and singing at the piano with his stepbrother, Ricky Stanley, and his cousin Billy Smith and his wife, Elvis and Ginger went to bed at about 05:00.

Unable to sleep, Elvis took some sleeping pills and, at 09:30, went to the bathroom with a book.

It was early afternoon before Ginger found Elvis' body lying on the floor in front of the toilet.

At 14:56 Elvis was rushed to the Baptist Medical Center in Memphis.

Elvis Presley was pronounced dead at 15:00.

At 16:00 Elvis' father, Vernon, told the world, "My son is dead."

The King is buried in the Meditation Garden at Graceland, but many conspiracy theorists believe that he is still alive today.

ELVIS' LAST CONVERSATION

AUNT DELTA

"Don't fall asleep in there."

ELVIS

"Okay, I won't."

MICHAEL JACKSON

1958–2009

Acclaimed American entertainer, singer, and songwriter Michael Jackson began a successful career as a member of family pop group *The Jackson 5*. Jackson shared a last meal with his children on June 24 before rehearsing for his forthcoming tour. Jackson returned home, but died on June 25, 2009, at his Neverland Mansion in Santa Barbara, California.

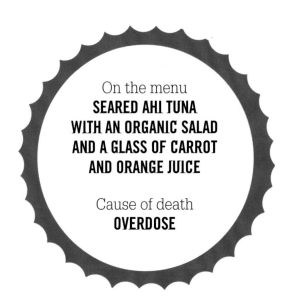

On the menu
**SEARED AHI TUNA
WITH AN ORGANIC SALAD
AND A GLASS OF CARROT
AND ORANGE JUICE**

Cause of death
OVERDOSE

FAVORITE DESSERT
Carrot pie with butter cream and cookies with chocolate and banana cream

FAVORITE RESTAURANT

Kentucky Fried Chicken

With estimated sales of over 400 million records worldwide, Michael Jackson was one of the most successful recording artists of all time.

Jackson won hundreds of accolades, making him the most-awarded recording artist in the history of popular music.

On what would have been Jackson's 52nd birthday, on August 29, 2010, he became the most downloaded artist in history.

Jackson constantly traveled the world to attend events honoring humanitarianism. *Guinness World Records 2000* recognized him for his support of 39 charities.

JIMI HENDRIX

1942-1970

Talented American guitarist, singer, and
songwriter Jimi Hendrix was the
ultimate rock star.

Hendrix was taken ill at the Samarkand Hotel,
London, on September 18, 1970, having spent
the evening with Monika Dannemann.

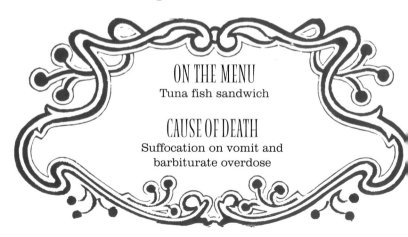

ON THE MENU
Tuna fish sandwich

CAUSE OF DEATH
Suffocation on vomit and
barbiturate overdose

Also known as Mama Cass, Elliot was an American singer and member of *The Mamas & the Papas* before becoming a successful solo artist.

Cass Elliot

1941-1974

Possibly a ham sandwich

CAUSE OF DEATH
Heart attack

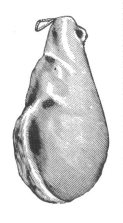

There is a cruel, but often repeated urban legend, that Mama Cass choked to death on a ham sandwich. This story began circulating after her body was discovered and police told reporters that a partially eaten sandwich had been found in her room and might have been to blame for her untimely death. An autopsy had yet to be conducted at this time.

However, the official post-mortem examination found that Elliot had suffered a heart attack, probably caused by recent extreme weight loss from fasting. No food at all was found in her windpipe.

Liberace

1919   1987

Wladzui Valentino Liberace was a child
musical prodigy and went on to become
a famous American pianist and vocalist.

Liberace opened the Liberace Museum
in 1978 to exhibit some of his cars,
pianos, costumes, and jewelry.

He died on February 4, 1987,
in Palm Springs, California.

ON THE MENU

cream of wheat
cereal with brown sugar

CAUSE OF DEATH
Pneumonia

Stephen Gately

1976–2009

ON THE MENU
WINE, CHAMPAGNE, AND CANNABIS

Stephen Patrick David Gately was an Irish singer with the pop group *Boyzone*.

Gately died on October 10, 2009, at his villa in Port d'Andratx, on the island of Mallorca.

CAUSE OF DEATH
PULMONARY EDEMA AS A RESULT OF AN UNDIAGNOSED HEART CONDITION

KURT COBAIN

1967–1994

American musician Kurt Cobain was perhaps best known as the lead singer of grunge band *Nirvana*. One of the last times he was seen in public was while dining at the *Cactus* restaurant, which serves southwestern American cuisine,in Madison Park, Seattle. He died at home on April 5, 1994.

ON THE MENU

It's rumored that his last meal was a can of root beer and some Camel Lights.

CAUSE OF DEATH

Suicide by gunshot

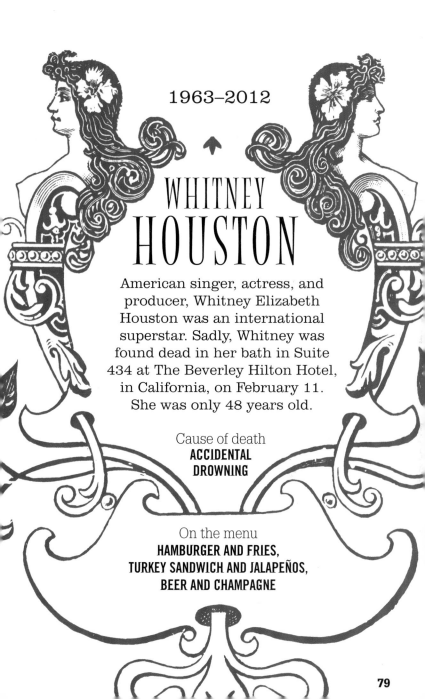

1963–2012

WHITNEY HOUSTON

American singer, actress, and producer, Whitney Elizabeth Houston was an international superstar. Sadly, Whitney was found dead in her bath in Suite 434 at The Beverley Hilton Hotel, in California, on February 11. She was only 48 years old.

Cause of death
ACCIDENTAL DROWNING

On the menu
HAMBURGER AND FRIES, TURKEY SANDWICH AND JALAPEÑOS, BEER AND CHAMPAGNE

Johann Schobert

1735–1767

German composer and harpsichordist Johann Schobert held a dinner party for friends on August 28, 1767, at his home in Paris.

Despite warnings from his guests, he asked for some mushrooms to be served. Unfortunately, they were poisonous.

Schobert, his wife, one of their children, a maid, and four friends all died as a result.

ON THE MENU

Mushrooms

CAUSE OF DEATH

Poisoning

MICHAEL HUTCHENCE

 **1960–1997**

Michael Kelland John Hutchence was an Australian musician and actor. He was a founding member and also the lead singer of rock band INXS from 1977 until his death in 1997.

Hutchence was found dead in Room 524 at the Ritz-Carlton hotel in Sydney, Australia. His death was later declared a suicide as a result of depression while under the influence of alcohol and drugs.

His body was discovered by a hotel maid, probably in a kneeling position facing the door. He had apparently used a snake-skin belt to tie a knot to the automatic closure at the top of the door and had strained his head forward into the loop so hard that the buckle had broken.

ON THE MENU

Indian curry

CAUSE OF DEATH
Suicide while under
the influence of alcohol and drugs

> "AFTER A GOOD DINNER ONE
> CAN FORGIVE ANYBODY, EVEN ONE'S
> OWN RELATIONS."
>
> OSCAR WILDE
> (FROM , 1893)

WRITERS

& LITERARY FIGURES

❦ ❦ ❦ ❦ ❦ ❦ ❦ ❦ ❦ ❦ ❦ ❦ ❦ ❦ ❦

FROM ERNEST HEMINGWAY'S HEARTY STEAK
AND POTATOES TO JULIA CHILD'S SIMPLE
FRENCH ONION SOUP, THIS CHAPTER TAKES A
PEEK INTO THE OFTEN TROUBLED LIVES OF
SOME OF THE WORLD'S MOST FAMOUS POETS,
PLAYWRIGHTS, AND NOVELISTS.

❦ ❦ ❦ ❦ ❦ ❦ ❦ ❦ ❦ ❦ ❦ ❦ ❦ ❦ ❦

LITERARY FOOD FACTS

FAVORITE HANGOUTS OF LITERARY GIANTS

BLUE BAR AT THE ALGONQUIN HOTEL, NEW YORK
Dorothy Parker, George S. Kauffman

OAK BAR, NEW YORK
F. Scott Fitzgerald

WHITE HORSE TAVERN, NEW YORK
Dylan Thomas, Hunter S. Thompson, Norman Mailer

CHUMLEY'S, NEW YORK
John Steinbeck, Ernest Hemingway, William Faulkner

McSORLEY'S OLD ALE HOUSE, NEW YORK
E. E. Cummings

MORE FAVORITE HANGOUTS OF LITERARY GIANTS

THE EAGLE AND CHILD, OXFORD, ENGLAND
J.R.R. Tolkien, C.S. Lewis

LA CLOSERIE DES LILAS, PARIS
Emile Zola, Oscar Wilde, Henry Miller

CERVECERIA, MADRID, SPAIN
Ernest Hemingway

TONERS, DUBLIN
W.B. Yeats, Patrick Kavanagh

WRITERS WHO CHOKED TO DEATH

CHRISTY BROWN (1932–1981)
Irish author, poet, and novelist who choked eating a lamb-chop meal.

TENNESSEE WILLIAMS (1911–1983)
American playwright who choked to death on a medicine-bottle cap while taking tranquilizers.

SHERWOOD ANDERSON (1876–1941)
American short-story writer who choked on a toothpick used to serve olives and hors d'oeuvres at a cocktail party on an ocean liner—this lead to fatal peritonitis.

Allen Ginsberg

1926–1997

American poet and contemporary of Jack Kerouc, William S. Burroughs, and other legends of the Beat Generation of the 1950s, Ginsberg was diagnosed with liver cancer in the late 1990s. He died in New York City after suffering a long illness. He is best known for his infamous book of poetry *Howl and Other Poems* (1956).

ON THE MENU

Fish chowder

Allen Ginsberg loved to make soup and served some friends a fish chowder soup a couple of weeks before he died. What remains of this soup has been frozen for posterity.

1899 ERNEST 1961
HEMINGWAY

On July 2, 1961, the American novelist Ernest Hemingway shot himself in the head after suffering from a bout of severe depression. He had already attempted to commit suicide in the spring of 1961, while at his home in Idaho. His acclaimed novels include *A Farewell to Arms* (1929), *For Whom The Bell Tolls* (1940), and *The Old Man and the Sea* (1952).

CAUSE OF DEATH
Suicide with a shotgun

ON THE MENU
New York strip steak
with baked potato
and a Caesar salad,
glass of Bordeaux

JULIA CHILD

1912–2004

Popular American chef, cookery writer, and television personality Julia Child wrote a wide range of cookery books, such as the two-volume classic *Mastering the Art of French Cooking* (1961 and 1970), which she co-authored with Simone Beck and Louisette Bertholle, and *Julia's Delicious Little Dinners* (1998). Child also appeared in numerous television programs championing cookery and good food, including a long-running series called *The French Cook* in the 1960s. The kitchen that made up the set for three of her television shows is now on display at the National Museum of American History in Washington, D.C.

More recently, Child provided inspiration for the book-turned-movie *Julie & Julia* (2009), which compares the life of Julia as a chef with that of a young New Yorker called Julie Powell who plans to cook all of the recipes in one of Julia's book in a year.

CAUSE OF DEATH Kidney failure

ON THE MENU

**A bowl of
French onion soup**

"It's fun to get together and have something good to eat at least once a day. That's what human life is all about—enjoying things."

On the day he died, Dylan Thomas reportedly said: "I've had 18 straight whiskies, I think that's the record."

1914–1953

DYLAN THOMAS

Perhaps most famous for *Under Milk Wood* (1954), Dylan Thomas was a talented Welsh poet of the twentieth century. Just as famous for his excessive drinking as for his mesmerizing and original poetry and prose, Thomas was a literary legend. Sadly, he became ill while drinking at a bar in Manhattan and fell into a coma, from which he never awoke. He died four days later at the age of 39.

ON THE MENU

Beer and whiskey

CAUSE OF DEATH Pneumonia, swelling of the brain, and a fatty liver

F. Scott Fitzgerald
1896–1940

A celebrated American novelist of the 1920s, F. Scott Fitzgerald died on December 21, 1940, at the Hollywood home of his friend Sheila Graham. They had visited the theater the night before. He is best known for his novel *The Great Gatsby* (1925).

Cause of death
Heart attack

On the menu

Candy bar from
Greenblatt's Deli,
Sunset Boulevard,
Hollywood

Anton Chekhov

1860   1904

Renowned Russian playwright
Anton Chekhov produced many
timeless literary works, including
The Seagull (1896) and
The Cherry Orchard (1904).

CAUSE OF DEATH

Tuberculosis

ON THE MENU

Champagne

"I HAVE BEEN UP TO CONGRESS
AND THEY DO NOT SEEM TO BE
ABLE TO DO ANYTHING EXCEPT TO
EAT PEANUTS AND CHEW TOBACCO,
WHILE MY ARMY IS STARVING."

ROBERT E. LEE
(ARMY GENERAL DURING THE
AMERICAN CIVIL WAR, 1861–1865)

ROYALTY

& OTHER HISTORICAL FIGURES

WITH POWER AND WEALTH AT THEIR DISPOSAL, MANY
ROYAL FIGURES, INCLUDING THE GLUTTONOUS GEORGE
IV OF BRITAIN, IRELAND, AND HANOVER, AND
FREDERICK OF SWEDEN, LED MERRY, CAREFREE
LIVES, ALTHOUGH ROYAL BLOOD DID NOT SPARE MANY
FROM MEETING TRAGIC ENDS. FIND OUT HOW FOOD
PLAYED A ROLE IN THE DEATHS OF VARIOUS ROYAL
FIGURES, ADVENTURERS, AND HEROES.

ROYAL FOOD FACTS

GLUTTONOUS MONARCHS & ARISTOCRATS

THE 3 KINGS

HENRY I
(1068–1135) NORMAN ENGLISH KING
WHO GORGED ON LAMPREY EELS,
ONLY TO DIE IN AGONY.

GEORGE IV
(1762–1830) BRITISH KING WHOSE HUGE CONSUMPTION
OF FOOD AND ALCOHOL LED TO OBESITY
AND PROBABLY HIS DEATH.

CHARLES I
(1500–1558) SPANISH KING AND HOLY ROMAN EMPEROR
WHO REGULARLY CONSUMED A WHOLE FOWL COOKED
IN MILK FOR BREAKFAST, A 20-DISH LUNCH
AT NOON, AND TWO SUPPERS, ONE AT 17:00
AND THE OTHER AT MIDNIGHT.

MELCHIOR DUKE OF BRUNSWICK-GRUBENHAGEN
(DIED C.1381)

GERMAN ARISTOCRAT WHO DIED AFTER EATING TOO MANY STRAWBERRIES

AN AVERAGE DAY FOR
HENRY VIII
WOULD INCLUDE:

3 LAMB CHOPS
2 CHICKEN LEGS
1 KILO OF BEEF
1 BOTTLE OF WINE
3 GLASSES OF BRANDY

The *Queen of Sheba* cake was originally a French chocolate cake known as *Gâteau de la Reine Saba*, named after the tenth-century-BCE African queen.

CORONATION CHICKEN

was invented for foreign guests at the Coronation of

QUEEN

ELIZABETH II, 1953

The following historical figures reputedly died from eating too many melons:

ALBERT II OF BOHEMIA
(1298–1358)

POPE PAUL II
(1417–1471)

FREDERICK III OF GERMANY
(1415–1493)

1755–1793

Marie Antoinette

ON THE MENU *Probably soup and vermicelli*

Queen of France

Born Archduchess of Austria, Marie Antoinette was the Queen of France from 1774 to 1792. As France sank into revolution, she became a target for hatred and resentment. Put on trial for treason against the French Republic, she was sentenced to death and executed at the Place de la Concorde on October 16, 1793.

CAUSE OF DEATH: *Execution by guillotine*

Princess
DIANA

1961 - 1997

ON THE MENU

For Diana: Mushroom and asparagus omelet
Dover sole with vegetable tempura

For Dodi: Grilled turbot
and Tattinger champagne

✳

CAUSE OF DEATH *Fatal car crash*

ON SUNDAY, AUGUST 31, 1997, PRINCESS DIANA, THEN THE MOST FAMOUS WOMAN IN THE WORLD, DIED IN A CAR CRASH WITH DODI FAYED IN THE PONTE D'ALMA TUNNEL, PARIS. AFTER EATING THEIR LAST MEAL AT *L'ESPADON*, A RESTAURANT IN THE RITZ HOTEL, THEY MADE THEIR FINAL JOURNEY BY CAR TO DODI'S PARISIAN APARTMENT.

Charles II

1630   1685

After living in exile during the English Civil War (1642–1651), Charles II became King of England in 1660, ushering in a period of merry-making and hedonism at the English court, which came as a welcome relief following the austerities of Oliver Cromwell and the Puritans' strict rule. Charles was on the throne when the Great Plague hit England in 1665 and the Great Fire almost destroyed London in 1666. He is famous for having many mistresses, including Nell Gwynne and Louise de Kérouaille, Duchess of Portsmouth.

ON THE MENU

A small amount of pottage (a type of thick soup), probably prepared for him by royal chef Giles Rose.

CAUSE OF DEATH **Apoplectic fit as a result of kidney dysfunction**

LAST WORDS: "You must pardon me, gentlemen, for being a most unconscionable time a-dying."

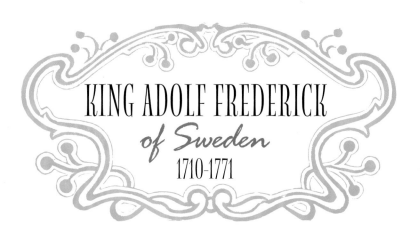

KING ADOLF FREDERICK
of Sweden
1710-1771

The eighteenth-century Swedish King Adolf was fond of his food. To celebrate 20 years on the throne, he held a sumptuous banquet at Stockholm Palace in which he consumed numerous servings of the main course and 14 servings of dessert. Not surprisingly, he died of digestive problems a few hours later.

CAUSE OF DEATH
Overindulgence and gluttony

ON THE MENU
Main course: Caviar, lobster, sauerkraut, and smoked herring, with champagne
Dessert: Sweet cream buns (known in Sweden as semla) and some warm milk

GEORGE PLANTAGENET

DUKE OF CLARENCE

1449-1478

ALTHOUGH CONFINED TO THE TOWER OF LONDON IN THE LATE 1400S, AND FACING EXECUTION BY BEHEADING FOR PLOTTING AGAINST HIS BROTHER, KING EDWARD IV, MANY BELIEVE THAT HE MAY HAVE BEEN DELIBERATELY DROWNED IN A BARREL OF WINE INSTEAD. HE DIED ON FEBRUARY 18, 1478.

GEORGE PLANTAGENET WAS IMPRISONED IN THE TOWER OF LONDON. IN ONE OF SHAKESPEARE'S PLAYS, TWO MEN ARE SENT TO MURDER HIM:

First Murderer "Take that, and that: if all this will not do, *Stabs him* I'll drown you in the malmsey-butt within." *Exit, with the body*

(SHAKESPEARE'S *THE LIFE AND DEATH OF RICHARD III*, ACT I, SCENE IV, LONDON, THE TOWER)

1869—1916

Rasputin

Grigori Yefimovich Rasputin, the son of a Russian peasant, became a trusted advisor to the Russian royal family—the Romanovs—in the early twentieth century. Reputed to have mystical powers, he gained the support of Empress Alexandra in 1908 when he demonstrated that he could control the Tsaravich Alexei's haemophilia. Many prominent Russians, including Prince Yusupov, felt Rasputin's influence was too far-reaching and plotted to murder him on December 29, 1916, in St. Petersburg.

CAUSE OF DEATH
Assassination—Rasputin was poisoned, shot, beaten, and then eventually drowned in the Neva River.

DID RASPUTIN FORSEE HIS DEATH?
"When the bell tolls three times, it will announce that I have been killed. If I am killed by common men, you and your children will rule Russia for centuries to come; if I am killed by one of your stock, you and your family will be killed by the Russian people! Pray, Tsar of Russia. Pray."

ON THE MENU

Honeyed cakes and Madeira wine (both poisoned with potassium cyanide)

The Romanov Royal Family

Executed en masse   **1918**

Emperor Tsar Nicholas II,
his wife Alexandra, and their
five children—Olga, Maria, Tatiana,
Anastasia, and Alexei—were held
prisoner after the people of the Russian
Revolution overthrew the Romanov
monarchy. When the Bolsheviks came to
power in October 1917, the Romanovs
were imprisoned in a country house at
Yekaterinburg where they were treated
harshly and eventually put to death. On July
16, 1918, the royal family and some of their
servants were gunned down in a basement.
As the smoke from the
rifles cleared, those who had survived
the initial shooting were stabbed to death
with bayonets.

ON THE MENU

The Romanovs
were placed on soldiers' rations on March 1, 1918
(having to give up luxuries such as butter and coffee)

CAUSE OF DEATH Assassination

GENERAL GEORGE ARMSTRONG CUSTER
1839–1876

An American soldier who demonstrated great courage during the American Civil War, fighting for the Union Army and helping to defeat the Confederate South. Custer met his death at the hands of Sioux, Cheyenne, and Arapaho Native Americans at the Battle of Little Bighorn in Montana on June 25-26, 1876. The battle is often referred to as "Custer's Last Stand." Custer had a private cook, Eliza Davidson, who traveled everywhere with him, even when he was about to go into battle!

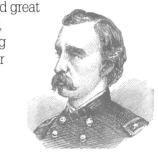

CAUSE OF DEATH **Died in battle**

ON THE MENU
ROASTED BUFFALO STEAKS, BEANS WITH MOLASSES, ROASTED WILD CORN, AND PRAIRIE HEN

ROBERT E. LEE

1807-1870

ON THE MENU
BEEF SOUP AND BRANDY

American army officer Robert E. Lee commanded the Confederate Army of Northern Virginia during the American Civil War (1861–1865). As the northern Union gradually defeated the southern states, Lee was finally forced to surrender to General Grant at Appomattox Court House in 1865.

CAUSE OF DEATH
LEE SUFFERED A STROKE ON SEPTEMBER 28, BEFORE DYING TWO WEEKS LATER OF PNEUMONIA.

HARRY HOUDINI

1874-1926

Originally from Hungary, the American illusionist, escapologist, and magician known as Houdini wowed the world with his feats of courage, fearless stunts, and escape acts. While appearing at the Garrick Theater in Detroit, Houdini fell very ill, but continued the performance in spite of a raging temperature and severe abdominal pains. Eventually, he was taken to hospital where he was diagnosed with a ruptured appendix. Houdini ate very little in the last week of his life, but Dr. Daniel Cohn, who was attending him, revealed that he asked for a special salad popular with Eastern European immigrants. Houdini fought death to the end, but finally escaped life's shackles on October 31, 1926.

CAUSE OF DEATH Acute appendicitis

ON THE MENU

FARMER'S CHOP SUEY (A SALAD OF LETTUCE, RADISH, CUCUMBER, CARROT, TOMATO, AND SCALLIONS/SPRING ONIONS WITH A SOUR CREAM AND COTTAGE CHEESE DRESSING)

Bonnie
and Clyde

Infamous outlaws, lovers, and partners-in-crime, Bonnie Parker (1910–1934) and Clyde Barrow (1909–1934) enjoyed a two-year crime spree during America's Great Depression.

They were eventually ambushed after having had breakfast at a café in Gibsland, Louisiana. They died in their Ford V-8 under a hail of bullets at 09:10 on May 23, 1934.

ON THE MENU

Breakfast at an American café (now the Bonnie and Clyde Ambush Museum)

HIDDEN TALENT!

Bonnie Parker wrote a small collection of poems called *Poetry from Life's Other Side* while in prison in 1932.

CAUSE OF DEATH

Ambushed and fatally shot near Louisiana Highway 154

Amelia Earhart

1897–1937

ON THE MENU
Possibly fish,
turtles,
and birds

CAUSE OF DEATH
Exact cause
unknown

In 1937, legendary female aviator Amelia Earhart disappeared over the Pacific Ocean while attempting to fly around the world. It is now believed she may have survived on fish and birds for weeks, or even months, on the remote Nikumaroro Island in the South Pacific.

ADMIRAL LORD NELSON

1758–1805

Nelson was a British naval commander who became famous for his role in the Napoleonic Wars. One of his most celebrated victories was the destruction of Napoleon Bonaparte's fleet at the Battle of the Nile in 1798. Under his command, the Royal Navy gained supremacy over the French, leading to the British triumph at the Battle of Trafalgar in 1805. Although Nelson's victory saved Britain from a French invasion, he died during battle on October 21, 1805.

ON THE MENU

Celery and Stilton soup
on board HMS Victory

CAUSE OF DEATH
Shot through the left
shoulder by a French sniper
while standing on deck

Lord Nelson has had a number of food items named after him, including the Lord Nelson Apple, a dish of mutton cutlets, as well as an early-19th-century boiled sweet somewhat indelicately called Nelson's Balls.

Ancient Historical Figures

Tutankhamun

(c. 1341–1323 BCE)

When the tomb of the "Boy King" Tutankhamun was uncovered by Howard Carter on November 4, 1922, archaeologists also discovered remnants of his final meal, since Egyptians traditionally took a last meal to sustain them in the afterlife. The preserved meal included stuffed geese, roast leg of lamb, half sides of beef, and personalized jars of wine.

ON THE MENU

Pickled roast beef, two kinds of bread, and some red wine (according to analysis of Tutankhamun's mummified stomach)

CAUSE OF DEATH Uncertain. Tutankhamun may have died as a result of a chariot-riding injury, although many believe he was assassinated.

CLEOPATRA

Pharaoh of Egypt

c.69-30 BCE

Cleopatra is a mesmerizing historical figure who has captivated historians and writers through the centuries. A successful Egyptian ruler, she seduced the Roman leader Julius Caesar, by whom she had a son, Caesarian. She later fell in love with another important Roman, Mark Antony, forming a romantic and political alliance with him against Rome's new leader, Octavian. After the disastrous Battle of Actium, Mark Antony committed suicide, believing that Cleopatra had already killed herself. Cleopatra then took her own life.

ON THE MENU
Basket of figs containing
an asp, a venomous snale

CAUSE OF DEATH
Suicide on August 12, 30 BCE

"NOT UNTIL THE LAST FIVE MINUTES DID THE AWFUL REALIZATION COME THAT THE END WAS AT HAND. THE LIGHTS BECAME DIM AND WENT OUT, BUT WE COULD SEE. SLOWLY, EVER SO SLOWLY, THE SURFACE OF THE WATER SEEMED TO COME TOWARDS US. SO GRADUAL WAS IT THAT... IT SEEMED A DREAM. DECK AFTER DECK WAS SUBMERGED."

ROBERT W. DANIEL
(A PHILADELPHIA BANKER AND SURVIVOR OF THE TITANIC DISASTER, 1912)

DISASTERS

& FAMOUS EVENTS

MANY PEOPLE, INCLUDING THE POMPEIANS LIVING IN THE SHADOW OF MOUNT VESUVIUS, WHO WERE CAUGHT UP IN THE MOST FAMOUS CATASTROPHES IN WORLD HISTORY HAD LITTLE IDEA THAT THEY FACED IMPENDING DEATH. SADLY, THE PASSENGERS ON THE TITANIC PROBABLY DID REALIZE THAT THEY HAD EATEN THEIR VERY LAST MEAL AS THE GREAT SHIP SLOWLY SANK INTO THE NORTH ATLANTIC.

EVENT FOOD FACTS

The American War of Independence 1775–1783

On December 4, 1783, George Washington, first president of the United States, held a last official meal as commander-in-chief of the Continental Army to commemorate the end of the American War of Independence. The banquet took place in the Long Room at Fraunes Tavern, New York.

THIS IS WHAT THE GUESTS FEASTED ON:

FISH HOUSE PUNCH

CRAB CLAWS
WITH DILL MUSTARD SAUCE

PATÉ MAISON FRAUNCES

CHEDDAR BISCUITS

SORREL SOUP WITH SIPPETS

COLD POACHED STRIPED BASS
WITH CUCUMBER SAUCE

MUSHROOM PASTRY BEEFSTEAK
AND KIDNEY PIE

ROASTED LAMB WITH
OYSTER FORCEMEAT

BAKED SMOKED COUNTRY HAM

MADEIRA MOLDED WINE JELLY

YAM AND CHESTNUT PIPPINS

PILAU OF RICE RAGOO

FRENCH BEANS

SKILLET CRANBERRIES

WATERMELON PICKLES

PEAR HONEY

SALLY LUNN MOLDED
BUTTER PRINTS

CARROT TEA CAKE

TIPSY SQUIRE TANSY PIE

WHISKEY NUT BALLS

CHOCOLATE TRUFFLES

APPLES, HAZELNUTS, PEARS,
ALMONDS, GRAPES

TOBACCO

COFFEE AND MADEIRA PORT

American Civil War 1861–1865

Soldiers fighting for the Union Army (the northern states) and the Confederate Army (the southern states) may have received the following rations:

SALTED PORK, BEEF, OR BACON

HARDTACK (A DRIED BISCUIT THAT COULD BE SOFTENED WITH LIQUIDS SUCH AS COFFEE)

CUSH (BEEF AND CORNMEAL FRIED IN BACON GREASE)

DRIED PEAS OR BEANS (OR PEANUTS IN THE SOUTH)

FRESH OR DRIED VEGETABLES AND FRUIT

MOLASSES

RICE

COFFEE, TEA, AND SUGAR

MILK

World War One 1914–1918

Getting food, especially hot dishes, to the troops on a regular basis was difficult for both the British and German armies. Here is a sample of the rations the troops could expect in the trenches:

BRITISH SERVICEMEN

MACONCHIE'S MEAT STEW (WITH HARD BISCUITS)

BREAD, OATMEAL, OR FLOUR

BUTTER OR MARGARINE

CHEESE

JAM OR DRIED FRUIT

FRESH VEGETABLES

DRIED VEGETABLES

A PORTION OF CHOCOLATE

TEA

RUM OR PORTER

20oz TOBACCO (MAXIMUM ALLOWED)

GERMAN SERVICEMEN

BREAD, FIELD BISCUITS, OR EGG BISCUITS

POTATOES

FRESH VEGETABLES

DRIED VEGETABLES

British families would send food parcels containing cakes, chocolate, canned food, and tobacco to soldiers during World War One.

THE TITANIC

THE MOST FAMOUS ILL-FATED VOYAGE IN HISTORY... BUT THEY CERTAINLY FILLED THEIR BOOTS FIRST!

❊ ❊ ❊ ❊ ❊ ❊ ❊ ❊ ❊ ❊ ❊ ❊ ❊ ❊ ❊ ❊ ❊ ❊ ❊

ON APRIL 10,1912, RMS Titanic was the largest passenger steamer that had ever been built in the world when she embarked upon her maiden voyage from Southampton, England, to New York City. At 23:40, on April 14, 1912, after sailing for four days, the Titanic struck an iceberg. She sank at 02:20 the next morning. In total 1,517 people lost their lives in one of the most well-known and worst maritime disasters in history.
Amazingly, 706 people managed to survive.

❊ ❊ ❊ ❊ ❊ ❊ ❊ ❊ ❊ ❊ ❊ ❊ ❊ ❊ ❊ ❊ ❊ ❊ ❊

1,517 people lost their lives on the Titanic
130 1ST CLASS, 166 2ND CLASS, 536 3RD CLASS, 685 CREW

1ST CLASS PASSENGERS

4.14.1912

THERE IS ONLY ONE KNOWN SURVIVING MENU FROM THE FIRST CLASS DINING ROOM. IT WAS PROBABLY ONE OF THE PASSENGERS' LAST MEALS BEFORE TAKING A DIP IN THE ICY WATERS OF THE NORTH ATLANTIC.

FIRST COURSE: HORS D'OEUVRES

OYSTERS A LA RUSSE

SECOND COURSE: SOUPS

CONSOMME OLGA

CREAM OF BARLEY

THIRD COURSE: FISH

POACHED SALMON WITH MOUSSELINE SAUCE & CUCUMBERS

FOURTH COURSE: ENTRÉES

FILET MIGNONS LILI

SAUTE OF CHICKEN LYONNAISE

VEGETABLE MARROW FARCI

FIFTH COURSE: REMOVES

LAMB WITH MINT SAUCE

ROAST DUCKLING WITH APPLE SAUCE

SIRLOIN OF BEEF WITH CHATEAU POTATOES, GREEN PEAS, & CREAMED CARROTS

BOILED RICE

PARMENTIER & BOILED NEW POTATOES

SIXTH COURSE: PUNCH

PUNCH ROMAINE

SEVENTH COURSE: ROAST

ROAST SQUAB & CRESS

EIGHTH COURSE: SALAD

COLD ASPARAGUS VINAIGRETTE

NINTH COURSE: COLD DISH

PATE DE FOIE GRAS

CELERY

TENTH COURSE: SWEETS

WALDORF PUDDING

PEACHES IN CHARTREUSE JELLY

CHOCOLATE & VANILLA ECLAIRS

FRENCH ICE CREAM

ELEVENTH COURSE: DESSERT

ASSORTED FRESH FRUITS & CHEESES

AFTER DINNER

COFFEE

CIGARS

2ND CLASS PASSENGERS

4.14.1912

...THE SECOND CLASS PASSENGERS
ATE PRETTY WELL TOO...

ON THE MENU

CONSOMME

TAPIOCA

BAKED HADDOCK & SHARP SAUCE

CURRIED CHICKEN & RICE

SPRING LAMB WITH MINT SAUCE

ROAST TURKEY WITH
CRANBERRY SAUCE,
GREEN PEAS, & PUREED TURNIPS

BOILED RICE

BOILED & ROAST POTATOES

PLUM PUDDING

WINE JELLY

COCONUT SANDWICH

AMERICAN ICE CREAM

NUTS AND ASSORTED FRESH FRUIT

CHEESE AND BISCUITS

COFFEE

3RD CLASS PASSENGERS

4.14.1912

THE LAST MEAL EATEN BY THE PEOPLE IN THIRD CLASS WAS SIMPLER THAN THAT SERVED TO THE OTHER TWO CLASSES, ALTHOUGH FOR MANY IT WAS MUCH BETTER-QUALITY FOOD THAN THEY WERE USED TO EATING ON A DAILY BASIS. UNFORTUNATELY, JUST UNDER A QUARTER OF THIRD-CLASS PASSENGERS SURVIVED THE TRAGIC ACCIDENT THAT LATER BEFELL THE TITANIC.

ON THE MENU

RICE SOUP

FRESH BREAD

CABIN BISCUITS

ROAST BEEF WITH BROWN GRAVY,
SWEETCORN, & BOILED POTATOES

PLUM PUDDING & SWEET SAUCE

FRUIT

"CERTAINLY THERE WAS NO SAILOR WHO EVER SAILED SALT WATER BUT WHO SMILED—AND STILL SMILES—AT THE IDEA OF THE 'UNSINKABLE SHIP,'"

Commander Charles Herbert Lightoller
THE SECOND OFFICER IN COMMAND ON BOARD RMS TITANIC

THE 1937 HINDENBURG AIRSHIP DISASTER

Huge airships were a luxurious means of transport in the 1930s. On May 3, 1937, the 800-ft-(244-m) long German airship LZ 129 Hindenburg, which was emblazoned with the Nazi swastika, left Frankfurt, Germany, on its way across the Atlantic to New York. It was due to dock at the Lakeside mooring mast in New Jersey, just outside New York, on the evening of Thursday, May 6. However, as the huge airship docked, it suddenly burst into flames. Amazingly, only 35 of the 97 passengers and crew on board were killed, plus one ground crewman, Allen Hagaman, who died later of his injuries.

On the menu
Passengers on board airships ate in style.

BREAKFAST

Bread and Butter with Honey and Preserves

Eggs (boiled or in a cup)

Frankfurt Sausage

Ham and Salami

Cheese and Fruit

Coffee, Tea, Milk, Cocoa

DINNER

Beef Broth with Marrow Dumplings

Rhine Salmon à la Graf Zeppelin

Roast Gosling Meunière with Mixed Salad and Apple Sauce

Pears Condé with Chocolate Sauce

Coffee

Fresh Fruit

SUPPER

Pâté à la Reine

Roast Filet of Beef with Mixed Salad

Cheese and Fresh Fruit

Coffee

Cause of death Exploding hydrogen gas inside the airship—most of the victims died from burns or smoke inhalation, while others died leaping from the stricken airship.

LAST MEAL ON APOLLO 11 MISSION

THE APOLLO 11 SPACE MISSION PUT THE FIRST MEN ON THE MOON IN 1969—A MOMENTOUS EVENT IN WORLD HISTORY. APOLLO 11 REALIZED AMERICAN PRESIDENT JOHN F. KENNEDY'S AMBITION OF LANDING ON THE MOON BEFORE THE SOVIET UNION BY THE END OF THE 1960S.

MEAL A
BACON SQUARES
PEACHES
SUGAR COOKIE CUBES
PINEAPPLE-
GRAPEFRUIT DRINK

MEAL B
CREAM OF CHICKEN SOUP
BEEF STEW
DATE FRUITCAKE
GRAPE PUNCH

THE CREW INCLUDED COMMANDER NEIL ARMSTRONG, MICHAEL COLLINS, AND EDWIN ALDRIN, JR. LAUNCHING ON JULY 16, THEY LANDED ON THE MOON ON JULY 20 BEFORE SPENDING THREE DAYS RETURNING TO EARTH. ON JULY 24, 1969, THE FINAL DAY OF THE APOLLO 11 MISSION, THE ASTRONAUTS ATE TWO LAST MEALS BEFORE LANDING IN THE PACIFIC OCEAN.

Treacle Wave

1.15.1919

ON THE MENU—
Lots of sugary treacle

CAUSE OF DEATH
Drowning

On January 15, 1919, disaster struck in Boston, in the United States, when a giant tank containing molasses (treacle) exploded on the site of the Purity Distilling Company. Just over three million gallons of molasses gushed into nearby streets, forming a giant wave that traveled at 35mph (56kph). Sadly, 21 people lost their lives and 150 people were injured. The wave even destroyed a fire station.

THE IRISH POTATO FAMINE

ON THE MENU
Rotten potatoes and decaying animals

CAUSE OF DEATH
Exposure, exhaustion, and starvation

In the nineteenth century, the Irish people found themselves in a desperate situation. A rising population and a shortage of land meant that they were increasingly reliant on growing and eating potatoes. In the south and west of Ireland, potatoes and milk were the staple diet.

When potato blight decimated the potato crops of 1845–1848, the Irish suffered terrible hardship and hunger. Around one million people died as a result of the famine.

ERUPTION OF
MOUNT VESUVIUS

✼ ✼ ✼ ✼ ✼ ✼ ✼ ✼ ✼ ✼ ✼ ✼ ✼

ON AUGUST 24, 79CE, Mount Vesuvius, the volcano that loomed over the ancient towns of Pompeii and Herculaneum, near Naples, Italy, erupted unexpectedly, raining down clouds of volcanic ash, pumice, and gases onto the hapless residents below. Scientific analysis of the contents of a cesspit in Pompeii has provided fascinating insights into the types of food enjoyed by the town's inhabitants.

ON THE MENU

Common Roman foods:
Chicken, fish (including lobster, squid, octopus, whitebait, and sea urchins), dormice, snails, eggs, cheese, beans, lentils, chickpeas, oats, bread, honey, cake, walnuts, almonds, pomegranates, peaches, grapes, pears, figs, olives, and wine

CAUSE OF DEATH Suffocation and exposure to an intense heat that burned victims' lungs

Soup Anyone?

ON THE MENU
HUMAN
SOUP

CAUSE OF DEATH
SICKNESS,
STARVATION,
AND
POSSIBLY
CANNIBALISM

In 1846, when a group of American pioneers—known as the Donner-Reed party—embarked on a journey from Illinois to California by wagon train, little did they know of the horrors awaiting them. Becoming trapped for months by heavy snowfall in the Sierra Nevada and taking a different route to the one planned, they were forced to eat their livestock and pets, as well as soup made from animal hides. Although there are conflicting accounts, it has been suggested that some of the pioneers had to resort to eating the flesh of their dead fellow travelers. Out of the 87 people who began that fateful journey, 48 were rescued by February 1847.

Captain Scott's
Antarctic Expedition
1910–1912

ON THE MENU

At the Cape Evans hut: Roast beef and Yorkshire pudding, seal meat, penguin breast, turtle soup, fresh bread, rhubarb pie, Buzzard cake, crystallized ginger, wine, and champagne.

ON THE MENU

While sledging:
Hoosh—a stew made from pemmican (a concentrated mixture of meat and fat) and biscuits, often with added raisins and arrowroot. This was before the food supplies ran out.

In an ill-fated attempt to be the first to reach the south pole, Captain Robert Falcon Scott and his men endured terrible weather and appalling conditions, including frostbite, snow blindness, starvation, and exhaustion from pulling heavy sledges.

Although, at times, their diet seemed good, poor nutrition and inadequate calories took their toll on the struggling men. On January 17, 1912, Scott and four other men reached the south pole. Facing an arduous return journey, Scott and his remaining men, Edward Wilson and Henry Bowers, all perished in their tent by March 29th.

Wonder drink: Scott's party drank lime juice on the expedition to ward off scurvy.

CAUSE OF DEATH **Starvation, hypothermia, and exhaustion**

CAPTAIN LAWRENCE OATES' FINAL BRAVE WORDS:
"I AM JUST GOING OUTSIDE. I MAY BE SOME TIME."

Authors' Acknowledgments

First and foremost, we would like to thank Cindy Richards and the lovely team at Cico—including Sally Powell and Pete Jorgensen—for giving us the opportunity to write this book. A very special thanks goes to Pete Jorgensen who saw its potential from the start; thank you, Pete!

To verify accuracy, we have cross-referenced the information in the book over as many sources as possible. However, as you travel into the distant past, what people ate before they died becomes more and more difficult to corroborate. So, apologies in advance for any errors of fact.

We would also like to say a big thank you to en.wikipedia.org (and its many contributors) whose website has proved an endless source of information on this morbidly fascinating subject and to the Death Penalty Information Center (DPIC) for its facts and figures on the death penalty in the United States (if you'd like to find out more, then visit www.deathpenaltyinfo.org).

Finally, we cannot fail to acknowledge the deceased themselves, both obscure and notorious, without whom this book could never have been written.